TO MY BEAUTIFUL
Daughter-in-Law

———————————

To My Daughter,

_____

_____

_____

_____

_____

_____

_____

_____

_____

_____

_____

_____

_____

_____

_____

_____

_____

_____

_____

I love you

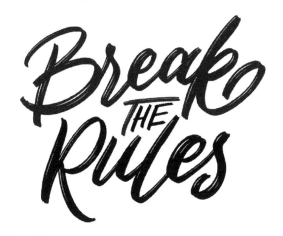

Daughter, live on the edge of adventure...

_____

_____

_____

_____

_____

_____

_____

_____

_____

_____

_____

NOTES & REMINDERS:

whatever
you are,
be a
good one

NOTES & REMINDERS:

live
MORE
worry
LeSS

Notes & Reminders

LIVE
&
lEARN

So there's a girl...
She stole my ♥ I am her
Mother-In-Law

Live
FOR
yourself

every moment matters

find your fire

LIVE & LEARN

shine bright

Reminder from Mom

be·a·voice·
not·an·
echo ♥

every moment matters

Like mother, like daughter

Reminder from Mom

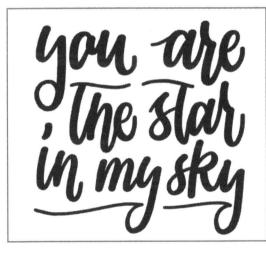
you are the star in my sky

_____

_____

_____

_____

_____

_____

_____

_____

_____

_____

_____

_____

Notes & Stuff

- BE -
YOU
- tiful -

_____

_____

_____

_____

_____

_____

_____

_____

_____

_____

THOUGHTS & REFLECTIONS

I'LL LOVE
YOU
forever
I'LL LIKE YOU
FOR
always
AS LONG
AS I'M LIVING
my
Baby
YOU'LL
BE.

live
MORE
worry
LeSS

_____

_____

_____

_____

_____

_____

_____

_____

_____

_____

NOTES:

REMINDERS:

Stars CAN'T SHINE WITHOUT Darkness

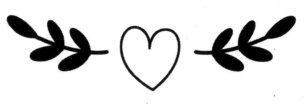

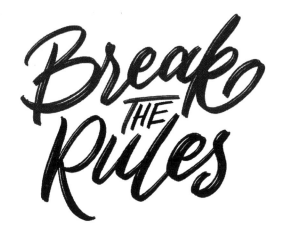

Daughter, live on the edge of adventure…

NOTES & REMINDERS:

whatever you are, be a good one

NOTES & REMINDERS:

live
MORE
worry
LeSS

Notes & Reminders

LIVE & learn

So there's a girl...
She stole my ♥ I am her
Mother-In-Law

Live
FOR
yourself

every moment matters

find your fire

LIVE & LEARN

_____

_____

_____

_____

_____

_____

_____

_____

_____

_____

_____

_____

Reminder from Mom

every moment matters

smile is the BEST make up

Like mother, like daughter

_____
_____
_____
_____
_____
_____
_____
_____
_____
_____
_____
_____

Reminder from Mom

_____

_____

_____

_____

_____

_____

_____

_____

_____

_____

_____

Notes & Stuff

_____

_____

_____

_____

_____

_____

_____

_____

_____

_____

THOUGHTS & REFLECTIONS

I'LL LOVE
YOU
forever
I'LL LIKE YOU
FOR
always
AS LONG
AS I'M LIVING
MY
Baby
YOU'LL
BE.

live
MORE
worry
LESS

_____

_____

_____

_____

_____

_____

_____

_____

_____

_____

NOTES:

REMINDERS:

Stars CAN'T SHINE WITHOUT Darkness

★ ★ ★

FAMILY
FAVORITE
Recipes

MOM'S KITCHEN
To Mine

BAKE TIME:

BAKE TEMP:

Ingredients

Directions

MOM'S KITCHEN
To Mine

BAKE TIME:

BAKE TEMP:

Ingredients

Directions

MOM'S KITCHEN
To Mine

BAKE TIME:

BAKE TEMP:

Ingredients

Directions

MOM'S KITCHEN
To Mine

BAKE TIME:

BAKE TEMP:

Ingredients

Directions

MOM'S KITCHEN
To Mine

BAKE TIME:

BAKE TEMP:

Ingredients

Directions

MOM'S KITCHEN
To Mine

BAKE TIME:

BAKE TEMP:

Ingredients

Directions

MOM'S KITCHEN
To Mine

BAKE TIME:

BAKE TEMP:

Ingredients

Directions

MOM'S KITCHEN
To Mine

BAKE TIME:

BAKE TEMP:

Ingredients

Directions

MOM'S KITCHEN
To Mine

BAKE TIME:

BAKE TEMP:

Ingredients

Directions